Book Cover Art

Book Covers are the introduction to your creative pages. Make them simple but eye-catching with pleasing color and embellishments.

Inside the cover is important too. Continue the theme throughout the book.

Time Cover

by Betsy McLoughlin

SUPPLIES: Clock print tissue paper • Game tiles to spell 'Time' • Miniature clock • Craft knife • Cutting mat • Ultimate glue

INSTRUCTIONS: Rip edges and crumple clock print paper. Smooth and glue on inside cover. Trace miniature clock on inside cover. Cut out shape with craft knife. Glue clock on first page. Glue several pages together behind clock for support. Make sure cover and pages close easily. Trim shape if necessary. Glue tiles in place.

Inside the Cover
Gold Book Cover

by Laurie Goodson

NOTE: You may wish to apply glaze to Brass eyelets to help hold them in place once they have been inserted. If you are using an older book and the cover is dirty or water stained, Lumiere paints are great for covering discolorations.

SUPPLIES: Light Brown and Plum cardstock • *Magenta* face stamp • Ancient Page Plum ink • Waxed linen thread • 3 large brass eyelets • Embellishments (coins, dominoes, poetry dog tags, crystals from chandeliers, beads, keys) • 2 yards of ⅜" Gold/Blue ribbon • Dremel tool with cutting disk and drill bit • Lumiere Bright Gold paint • Paintbrush • Diamond Glaze

INSTRUCTIONS: Using Dremel tool, cut small rectangle in front cover of book. Paint front and back covers and spine Bright Gold. Stamp face on Light Brown cardstock with Plum ink. Cut out image and glue on 1½" x 2½" piece of Plum cardstock. Glue face behind opening in front cover. Drill holes in top left corner and at center right edge of front cover and at center of outside edge of back cover. Insert eyelets in holes. Using linen thread, attach embellishments so they hang on outside of book from eyelet in upper left hand corner. Cut ribbon in half and tie pieces to front and back cover through eyelets using lark's head knots. Tie book closed with ribbon.

Since altered books are collaborative works of art, I prefer to leave my covers simple and focus on the closures. I like to have the surprises inside. There is nothing like placing an altered book on a coffee table and watching the way people are drawn to it. They know it is a book, yet somehow very different.

Lock & Key Cover

by Laurie Goodson

SUPPLIES: Gold decorative metal corners • Brass hinged latch and loop • Small Brass lock and key • 3" leather strap • Waxed linen thread • Gold fibers • Sewing needle • Awl • Diamond Glaze

INSTRUCTIONS: With awl, make 2 holes in leather strap aligning holes with nail holes on hinge. Using linen thread and needle, sew hinge to leather strap. Adhere metal loop and metal corners to front of book with Diamond Glaze, let dry. Place latch over loop, pull leather strap to back of book. Make 2 holes through leather strap and back of book. Make sure strap is long enough for thickness of book once inside art is complete. You may prefer to attach strap and latch after you have completed book to make sure there are no problems with closure. Insert lock in loop. Tie fibers in hole in key and insert key in lock.

More Cover Art

Woven Fibers Cover

by Betsy McLoughlin

SUPPLIES: Rust cardstock • Photo • Rubber stamps (*Uptown Design* 'serendipity', dot background) • Sepia ink • Black ink pad • Assorted fibers • 3" square of plastic mesh • Small piece of Gold mesh ribbon • PSX music instrument stickers • 2 buttons • Gold cord • Assorted beads • 2 Black eyelets with washers • 4 Gold photo corners • Eyelet setter • Hammer • 1/8" hole punch • Lumiere Super Copper paint • Foam paintbrush • Ultimate glue

INSTRUCTIONS: Paint cover Super Copper. Weave fibers through plastic mesh. Tie beads on ends of fibers. Glue woven mesh on cover.

Cut cardstock to fit inside cover and extending over first page. Glue cardstock on inside cover. Fold back to create a pocket as shown. Punch holes in bottom of fold and attach washers and eyelets. Attach Gold cord through one eyelet. Glue small button on page, let dry. Glue large button on top of small button, let dry. Wrap cord around button to secure edge of pocket. Apply stickers, ribbon and stamp word with Black ink.

On page behind pocket, stamp dot background with Sepia ink.

Attach photo with photo corners.

Lark's Head Knot for Bookmark and Red Cover

Bookmark
by Laurie Goodson

SUPPLIES: Manila tag • Fiber • PSX music stickers • Mica tile • Gold glitter • Gold leafing pen • Clear embossing powder • Heat gun • 1 9/16" square punch • 1/4" hole punch • Glue

INSTRUCTIONS: Cut out page with book title and trim to fit tag. Punch square window. Separate flakes of mica tile, apply sticker and small amount of glitter, sprinkle with embossing powder. Place mica tile on top. Heat with heat gun to melt powder and seal tile. Place mica window in punched window, glue to secure. Glue paper piece on tag. Punch hole in top of tag, attach fiber and apply stickers. Edge with leafing pen and place in pocket.

Red Cover
by Laurie Goodson

SUPPLIES: Old piece of Silver jewelry • Button • Decorative Silver corners • Small flat key • Black elastic ponytail band • Diamond Glaze

INSTRUCTIONS: On front cover, adhere corners and button with glaze, let dry. Use glaze to attach piece of jewelry to top of button for clasp. On back cover, adhere key with glaze. Make sure the hole on top of the key extends over the edge. Tie elastic though the hole in the key with a lark's head knot. Pull the elastic to front and wrap around jewelry piece to close book.

The sweet little angel on this book came from a candlestick holder. It had a flat back and two screws for mounting. Instead of a traditional clasp, the weight of the angel will help keep the book from bulging too much. When you attach a three-dimensional piece to a book cover with screws, you can take it off when you need to work inside the book.

Angel Cover
by Laurie Goodson

SUPPLIES: Music print paper • Decorative metal corners • 5" resin angel • Dremel tool with drill bit • Screwdriver • Screws • Diamond Glaze

INSTRUCTIONS: Determine where you want to mount angel and mark screw placement on cover. Drill holes in cover. Line inside of book cover with music print paper. Mount angel on cover with screws. Using Diamond Glaze, glue metal corners on corners of cover.

Eyes Pages

by Betsy McLoughlin

SUPPLIES: Magazine pictures • Acetate sheet • Dr. Ph. Martin calligraphy inks • Paintbrush • Craft knife • Laser printer • Glue stick

INSTRUCTIONS: Paint inks on page in random pattern leaving some words showing. On opposite page, draw old fashioned window. Cut out window with craft knife. Find magazine picture with sky and glue on next page. On computer, type saying and print on acetate. Glue saying on back of window. Glue entire page down. Cut pictures of eyes from magazine and glue in place.

Add Paint on Pages

with Direct to Paper Technique

Paint is a brilliant way to add visual interest and vibrant color to any page. Remember… there are no rules!

Applying Ink - Using the Direct to Paper Technique

This technique is how stampers 'paint', and the end results can be very dramatic. The only rule is that there are no rules!

Using an ink pad, begin by making different 'swooshing' motions on paper. You can obtain different results by using different strokes. A Cats Eye pad will make a stroke similar to a brush, a Petal Point pad combines a fine point and a rounded end, and a rectangular pad is good for just skimming over the paper surface. You can use the entire sponge surface or the tip or edge. The movement of your hand will create a texture or pattern. Alter the direction of strokes. Each direction pushes the ink in new ways.

If you get too much ink on a project, smear it with a paper towel, blend it with a make-up sponge or blot it on a placemat.

Bottled inks can be applied with a sponge or sponge brush.

As this technique has grown and expanded, I've learned that one can use a variety of inks and ink pads on a variety of papers. I recommend experimenting to discover what works best for you and the particular piece of art you are coloring.

1. Mask desired words with correction tape.

2. Color page using a sponge.

3. Let paint dry and remove correction tape.

4. Apply more paint directly to page using a sponge.

Renaissance Woman & Gold

by Betsy McLoughlin

SUPPLIES: Greeting cards print paper • Color copy of artwork • Gold spray paint • Matte finish spray • Xyron machine • Glue

INSTRUCTIONS: Spray paint right page Gold, let dry. Spray matte finish over Gold to seal, let dry. Run artwork through Xyron machine and adhere to left page. Trim off excess. Cut greeting cards from paper and glue as shown.

Clock Face Pages

by Betsy McLoughlin

SUPPLIES: White cardstock • Rubber stamps (*A Stamp In The Hand* clock face with wings, *Art Impressions* time, face in a circle) • Nick Bantock Black ink pad • Tsukineko All Purpose inks • Self-adhesive clock numbers • Gold decorative braid • Fantastix applicators • Ultimate glue

INSTRUCTIONS: Glue cardstock on facing pages. Stamp face with Black on left page and color with applicators. Remove backing and adhere clock numbers over stamped image. Stamp 'time' on scrap paper, tear out and glue under clock. On opposite page, apply All Purpose Inks in random pattern with applicators. Stamp 'time' and face with wings using All Purpose ink. Glue trim around words.

Purple & Green Pages

by Betsy McLoughlin

SUPPLIES: Architectural print decorative paper • Cat's Eye ink pads • Dye based ink pads • Assorted fibers • Lumiere Halo Pink Gold paint • Paintbrush • 1/8" hole punch • Varnish • Ultimate ink

INSTRUCTIONS: Paint left page Halo Pink Gold. Trim opposite pages in zig zag pattern with scissors. For Purple and Blue page, fold page in half and glue. Using direct to paper technique, apply Purple dye based ink pad on one side and Blue on other side. Glue decorative paper on next page. Apply Purple, Green and Blue Cat's Eye inks. Apply varnish over inks, let dry. Punch holes down side of left page and lace with fibers.

Choose images that you like and combine them in a collage that zings with excitement, fun and color.

Follow the easy steps below!

Creating the Collage Page

1. Paint the page Gold using a good paintbrush.

2. Tear out the desired words and phrases.

3. Glue the lips and cut-out words on the page.

Lips Page
by Betsy McLoughlin

SUPPLIES: Magazine pictures and words • Lumiere Metallic Gold paint • Diamond glaze • Clear holeless beads • Paintbrush • Glue stick

INSTRUCTIONS: Paint page Metallic Gold, let dry. Cut out pictures of lips and words. Cut out some words and rip others. Glue the images on page. Apply diamond glaze in small areas of page and add Clear beads.

Creating the Pocket Page

1. Stamp the phrase on the vellum.

2. Attach eyelet to tag.

Rose Pocket Page
by Betsy McLoughlin

SUPPLIES: Rose print paper • Vellum • Emerson quote rubber stamp • Black Lightning ink pad • White pearls by the yard • Pink tassel • Pink eyelet • Gold glitter spray • Cutting mat • Craft knife • Eyelet setter • Hammer • 1/8" hole punch • Decorative scissors • Xyron machine • Glue stick • Ultimate glue

INSTRUCTIONS: Run rose paper through Xyron machine, adhere to page, trim excess with craft knife and cutting mat. For pocket, trim rose paper around flower petals. Glue on page. Stamp phrase on vellum, let dry. Run through Xyron machine, attach to rose paper and cut with decorative scissors. Punch hole in corner of tag and attach eyelet. Thread tassel and pearls through eyelet. Spray page with glitter. Glue pearls in crease. Place tag in pocket.

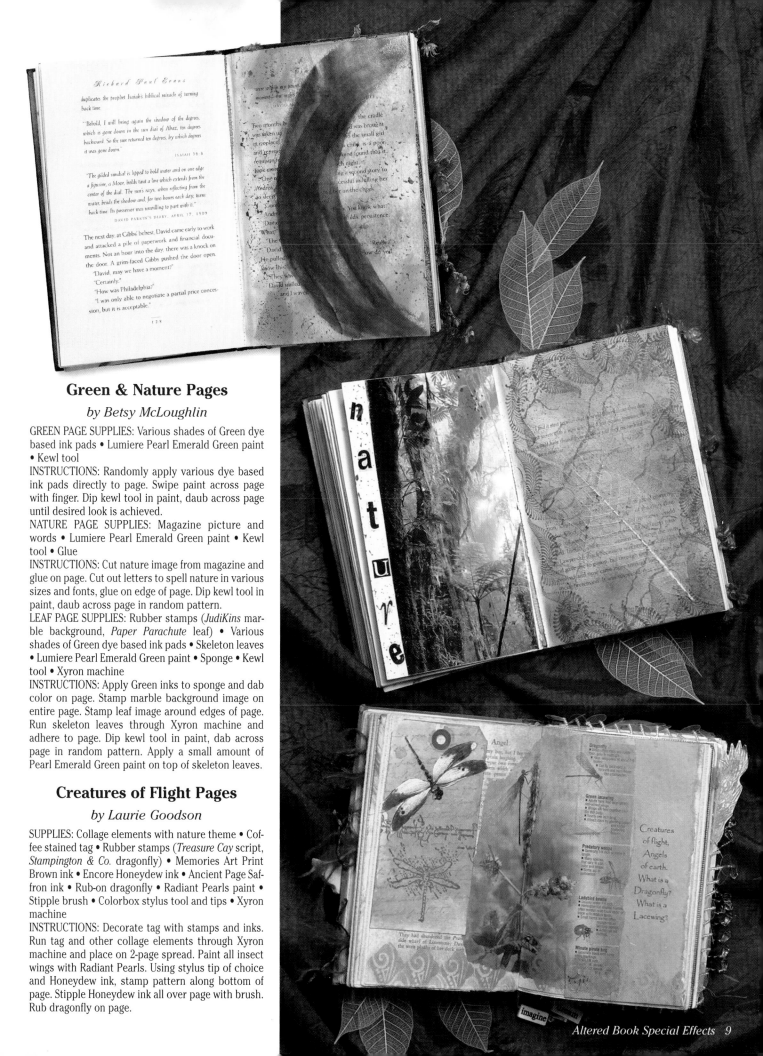

Green & Nature Pages

by Betsy McLoughlin

GREEN PAGE SUPPLIES: Various shades of Green dye based ink pads • Lumiere Pearl Emerald Green paint • Kewl tool

INSTRUCTIONS: Randomly apply various dye based ink pads directly to page. Swipe paint across page with finger. Dip kewl tool in paint, daub across page until desired look is achieved.

NATURE PAGE SUPPLIES: Magazine picture and words • Lumiere Pearl Emerald Green paint • Kewl tool • Glue

INSTRUCTIONS: Cut nature image from magazine and glue on page. Cut out letters to spell nature in various sizes and fonts, glue on edge of page. Dip kewl tool in paint, daub across page in random pattern.

LEAF PAGE SUPPLIES: Rubber stamps (*JudiKins* marble background, *Paper Parachute* leaf) • Various shades of Green dye based ink pads • Skeleton leaves • Lumiere Pearl Emerald Green paint • Sponge • Kewl tool • Xyron machine

INSTRUCTIONS: Apply Green inks to sponge and dab color on page. Stamp marble background image on entire page. Stamp leaf image around edges of page. Run skeleton leaves through Xyron machine and adhere to page. Dip kewl tool in paint, dab across page in random pattern. Apply a small amount of Pearl Emerald Green paint on top of skeleton leaves.

Creatures of Flight Pages

by Laurie Goodson

SUPPLIES: Collage elements with nature theme • Coffee stained tag • Rubber stamps (*Treasure Cay* script, *Stampington & Co.* dragonfly) • Memories Art Print Brown ink • Encore Honeydew ink • Ancient Page Saffron ink • Rub-on dragonfly • Radiant Pearls paint • Stipple brush • Colorbox stylus tool and tips • Xyron machine

INSTRUCTIONS: Decorate tag with stamps and inks. Run tag and other collage elements through Xyron machine and place on 2-page spread. Paint all insect wings with Radiant Pearls. Using stylus tip of choice and Honeydew ink, stamp pattern along bottom of page. Stipple Honeydew ink all over page with brush. Rub dragonfly on page.

Close-up Face Pages

by Laurie Goodson

SUPPLIES: Green textured paper • Color copy of a face • Fresco Olive Grove ink • Ruler • Xyron machine
INSTRUCTIONS: Rub Fresco ink directly on 2-page spread. Run image and textured paper through Xyron machine. Cut image into 1" squares. Cut nine 1" squares of textured paper. Adhere image on page leaving ¹/₁₆" gap between squares. Adhere textured squares around image to fill top and bottom of page.

Tiles & Mosaics

Cut out or punch shapes from paper and photos… then combine them for a mosaic effect.

1. Cut the image into 1" squares with scissors.

2. Assemble the squares on the page and glue in place.

Create Stripes with a Black & White Image and a Color Image

by Betsy McLoughlin

SUPPLIES: Color and Black and White copies of art • Craft knife • Cutting mat • Ruler • Xyron machine
INSTRUCTIONS: Run each copy of artwork through Xyron machine. Cut artwork into ½" strips. Apply alternating Black and White and color strips on pages.

Washi Paper Punched Page
by Betsy McLoughlin

SUPPLIES: Washi paper • Scrap paper • Oriental woman art • 4 Gold photo corners • 1" x 1¾" diamond punch • Craft knife • Cutting mat • Spray adhesive

INSTRUCTIONS: Punch diamonds from Washi paper. Since Washi paper is very thin, place a piece of scrap paper underneath for stability and ease of punching. Spray page with adhesive. Adhere punched shapes as shown. Trim excess around edges with craft knife and cutting mat. Attach woman to opposite page with photo corners.

Woman Pages
by Laurie Goodson

SUPPLIES: Black textured paper • Color copy of an image • Fresco Tuscan Earth ink • Paper cutter • Xyron machine • Paintbrush • Diamond Glaze

INSTRUCTIONS: Rub Fresco ink directly on 2-page spread of book. Run image and textured paper through Xyron machine. Using paper cutter, cut image into 1½" squares. Cut nine 1½" squares of Black textured paper. Assemble image on page leaving ¹⁄₁₆" gap between squares. Place Black squares around image to fill in page. Paint squares with glaze. Let dry over night

Persian Rug Page
by Betsy McLoughlin

SUPPLIES: Rug pictures from magazine • Craft knife • Ultimate glue

INSTRUCTIONS: Trim rugs to various sizes with craft knife. Apply glue and randomly place on page.

Windows & Doors

Continue a specific theme for several pages as we did with the Eiffel Tower Pages. Using windows and folds gives added appeal to your altered books.

Eiffel Tower Pages

by Laurie Goodson

SUPPLIES: Decorative text weight paper • Scrap of Tan paper • One medium shipping tag • Alphabet rubber stamps • Black ink pad • One reproduction luggage sticker • Old photo of Eiffel Tower • 4 Black photo corners • Four medium sized Brass brads • Craft knife • Cutting mat • Ruler • Xyron machine • Gel medium

INSTRUCTIONS: Cut decorative paper so it covers 1¼ book pages. Run paper through Xyron machine and apply to page. Using cutting mat, craft knife and ruler, cut an X in center of page. Fold back resulting triangles. Place a brad through each folded triangle to hold tab down. Stamp 'Paris' on Tan paper, tear around edges and glue on left page.

On page immediately following window page, fold corners down and in toward spine, glue. Attach luggage sticker to shipping tag. Glue tag on folded page so it shows through window on previous page.

On the next page, mount photo with photo corners.

Windows & Doors Pages

by Betsy McLoughlin

SUPPLIES: Navy Blue leather grain paper • Images of women • Assorted game tiles to spell 'open doors' • 2 decorative beads • Brass hinges and clasps • Craft knife • Cutting mat • Ruler • Xyron machine • Ultimate glue
INSTRUCTIONS: Decide on picture placement. Mark window placement on opposite pages. Run decorative paper through Xyron and adhere to pages. Cut out windows, glue pictures in place and glue pages together. Glue hinges, clasps and bead handles on windows. Glue tiles in place.

1. Mark the cutting lines using a pencil and ruler.

2. Place door area on a cutting mat, cut with craft knife.

3. Glue picture on the page behind doors or windows.

4. Glue the hinges in place.

Windows & Doors

*Cut-out windows and doors add movement and mystery to the books you alter...
"What will I find?"*

Niches & Doors

by Laurie Goodson

Niches and doors allow the inclusion of three-dimensional objects in your book design.

1. Mark the opening for the book niche.

2. Cut a niche using a craft knife and ruler.

3. Lift out the cut pages with tip of a craft knife.

4. Glue pages together with a glue stick.

5. Mark the positions for screw holes.

Hidden Treasures Pages

by Laurie Goodson

SUPPLIES: Tag • Coin envelope • Cream paper • *Treasure Cay* collage rubber stamp • Fresco Vatican Wine ink • Memories Art Print Brown ink • Lumiere paint (Metallic Gold, Super Copper) • Game letter tiles to spell ART • 2 small Brass hinges • Assorted fibers • Craft knife • Cutting mat • Decorative scissors • Gel medium

INSTRUCTIONS: Using craft knife, cut a rectangular hole in 35 pages of book. Glue pages together. Paint first uncut page following cut pages Super Copper, let dry. Rub Fresco ink on coin envelope and tag. Stamp image on envelope and tag using Art Print Brown ink. Glue one side of each hinge on coin envelope. Screw other sides of hinges into glued pages. Glue Copper painted page to cut pages. Glue 2 more uncut pages to back of the Copper page. Dab Metallic Gold paint on Scrabble tiles. Attach tiles in window with Gel medium. Tie fibers to tag with lark's head knot. Place tag inside coin envelope.

Print words on Cream paper. Rub with Fresco ink and cut out with decorative scissors. Glue on left page.

Frame & Dress Form Pages

by Laurie Goodson

SUPPLIES: Scrap text strips • Plastic doll dress form found in packaging of doll gowns • *Inkadinkado* rubber stamps (right and left wings, words) • Encore Blue Metallic ink • Memories Black ink • Seed beads • Iridescent beaded ribbon fringe • Lumiere paint (Pearl Blue, Pearl White) • Paint-

Frame & Dress Form Continued

brush • Craft knife • Cutting mat • Wonder Tape • Gel medium • Diamond Glaze

INSTRUCTIONS FOR FRAME: Place cutting mat behind 3 pages and cut rectangle out of the center. Repeat until 21 pages have been cut. Glue pages together with gel medium. Place tape around edge of window and press beads into tape.

INSTRUCTIONS FOR DRESS FORM: Apply glue to face of text strips and place randomly inside dress form so text can be read. Paint inside of dress form Pearl Blue and Pearl White. Place dress form in center of page behind window and trace around form with pencil. Place cutting mat behind page and cut out traced image with craft knife. Stamp wings on page above cut-out with Blue Metallic ink. Paint entire page immediately following cut-out with gel medium. Place dress form where it will come through cut-out. Press cut-out page and glued page together. Stamp Black words on cut-out page. Apply Diamond Glaze around dress form to seal. Let dry. Glue 2 following pages together with gel medium, then sandwich fringe between these pages and dress form page.

Square, diamond and rectangle niches and doors are wonderful ways to create interest and intrigue in art books.

1. Mark the opening, cut with a craft knife.

2. Fold flaps to back.

3. Attach the folds to the page with eyelets.

4. Glue a picture behind the opening.

Victorian Lady
by Betsy McLoughlin

SUPPLIES: Color copy of artwork • 4 Pine Green eyelets • Eyelet setter • Hammer • 1/8" hole punch • Craft knife • Bone folder • Ruler • Xyron machine • Ultimate glue

INSTRUCTIONS: Cut center of page in large cross shape. Use bone folder and ruler to fold back each edge of page. Punch holes in folded corners and attach eyelets. Run image through Xyron machine, center image in opening and adhere to page. Glue pages together. Trim flower from leftover image, adhere to bottom of page.

Harlequin Pages
by Laurie Goodson

SUPPLIES: Text tile beads • Black Sharpie pen • Black rattail cord • Ruler • Gel medium

INSTRUCTIONS: Using ruler and pencil, draw harlequin diamonds across 2-page spread. Do not try for precision. Fill diamonds with Black pen. Ink tends to bleed through, so be sure to put cutting mat or paper behind pages when you color. Create a sentence with text tile beads and string beads on cord. Tie knots on ends of cord. Glue tiles in place. Avoid getting glue on cord so that it will hang freely.

Color & Draw
with Word Play

Black geometric designs make dramatic statements and backgrounds for black and white photos and unusual embellishments. Remember, there are no rules to govern what you want to create. If you can think it… you can do it!

1. Draw diamonds on page using a pencil and ruler.

2. Color every other diamond with a permanent pen.

3. Make a sentence with word tiles, string on cord.

4. Glue the tile beads across the page.

Rubber stamps are a crafter's dream come true as shown in the Renaissance and Asian pages.

The designs were stamped and then adhered to the existing pages. What fantastic results!

by Betsy McLoughlin

Renaissance Pages

SUPPLIES: White cardstock • Rubber stamps (*Hero Arts* shadow, *Acey Deucy* man and woman) • Nick Bantock Black ink pad • Craft knife • Xyron machine • Foam tape

INSTRUCTIONS: Carefully remove 2 pages from book with craft knife. Stamp shadow using Black ink in a diagonal pattern on both pages. Run pages through Xyron machine. Adhere pages to book. Stamp man and woman images twice on White cardstock with Black ink and cut out. Run one set of people through Xyron machine and adhere to page facing each other. Apply foam tape to remaining set of people and adhere on top of first images.

Asian Pages

SUPPLIES: Washi paper • Black and White card-stock • *Stamps in Motion* Asian woman rubber stamp • White pigment ink • White embossing powder • Lumiere Metallic Silver paint • Black rat-tail cord • 4 Black eyelets and washers • Eyelet setter • Hammer • Hole punch • Heat gun • Paint-brush • Craft knife • Cutting mat • Xyron machine • Ultimate glue

INSTRUCTIONS: Paint left page Metallic Silver, let dry. Stamp woman on Black cardstock with White pigment ink and emboss with White embossing powder. Cut out image, glue on White cardstock. Punch holes for eyelets, set washers and eyelets in cardstock and painted page. Glue cord on edge of card and in crease of book.

For opposite page, run washi paper through Xyron machine, adhere to page and trim excess with craft knife and cutting mat.

Button collectors will love our Buttons page. Simply cut the shanks off the buttons and glue!

Buttons Page

SUPPLIES: Letters from magazines • Decorative buttons • Lumiere Pearl Blue paint • Old sharp scissors • Spray adhesive • Glue stick • Ultimate glue

INSTRUCTIONS: Select page in book and randomly trim edge of paper. Paint page Pearl Blue, let dry. Cut shanks off buttons with sharp scissors. After deciding on placement, apply glue to back of buttons and place on paper. Let glue dry. Cut out letters to spell buttons from various magazines varying the font size, style and color. Glue letters in place with glue stick. Glue painted page to page behind it with spray adhesive.

Open Doors

by Laurie Goodson

Architectural doors open to reveal words or sentiments that are close to your heart.

1. Glue door and script paper on book page.

2. Cut 3 sides of the door with a craft knife.

3. Glue vellum behind the door opening.

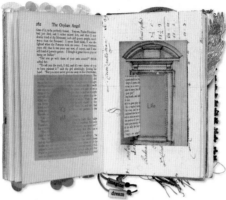

Many Door Pages

SUPPLIES: Five pieces of old script text weight paper cut to fit book pages • Five different architectural doors cut from printed text weight paper • Five 3½" squares of Gold vellum with computer generated words • Photo • 4 Gold photo corners • Brown acrylic paint • Craft knife • Cutting mat • Sponge • Xyron machine • Gel medium

INSTRUCTIONS: Run script paper and architectural doors paper through Xyron machine. Attach script paper to page. Attach door to center of page. Place cutting mat behind page, cut around door on 3 sides so it will open. Glue vellum behind door with gel medium. Repeat on next 4 pages. Sponge Brown paint on left page, let dry. Mount photo on page with photo corners.

I absolutely love this technique! It reminds me of my old children's books when I was little. I fondly remember a Snow White book that had a wheel. The possibilities are limitless.

Spinner Pages

SUPPLIES: Ivory cardstock • Acetate sheet • Rubber stamps (face, *Inkadinkado* word, *A Stamp in the Hand* eye, 2 *Hero Arts* words) • Fresco dye inks (Mediterranean Tide, Venetian Sunrise, Da Vinci Violet, Blue Grotto) • Black dye ink • Brass brad • 3 metal washers • Assorted fibers • Beaded fringe • ⅛" hole punch • 4" circle cutter • Craft knife • Cutting mat • Awl • Diamond Glaze • Gel medium

INSTRUCTIONS: Cut 4" cardstock circle. Cut two 1" acetate circles with circle cutter. Mark 4 equal size triangles on large circle. Mask and color each fourth with a different color of Fresco inks using direct-to-paper technique. With Black dye ink, stamp a different image in each section. Position word stamps so they read from center of circle out for legibility. Cut a window in a book page placed so it reveals a fourth of the circle. The top of circle should extend slightly above edge of page allowing it to turn. Mark window placement and center of circle. Using craft knife, cut window in book slightly smaller than a fourth of circle.

Punch a hole in center of each acetate circle with awl. Punch a hole through center of Ivory circle. Place one acetate circle on brad and press brad through center of circle. Place second acetate circle on brad behind page. Place larger decorated circle on brad. Fold brad down. Using gel medium, glue window page to page behind it along outside and bottom edges only. To allow for movement, do not glue too close to circle. Tie fibers to washers with lark's head knots. Using Diamond Glaze, adhere washers to page just below window. Glue fringe along edge of page. Stamp a face with Black ink on opposite page.

Moveable Wheel

by Laurie Goodson

Interactive pages are what altered books are all about. So, get in the action with a moveable wheel.

1. Cut out a circle and mark the divisions.

2. Trace a triangle section of circle on page and cut out.

3. Place circle behind opening and attach with a brad.

4. Glue beaded fringe down the page.

Violet Pages

SUPPLIES: Text weight paper • 7 Lavender flat back marbles • 8" of 3/8" Lavender ribbon • Small key • Lumiere Pearl Violet paint • 5/8" circle punch • Paintbrush • Diamond Glaze • 3M repositionable glue stick • Gel medium

INSTRUCTIONS: Punch 7 circles from text weight paper. Find seven words on page of book that you want to highlight. Using glue stick, place circles pages to mask words you chose. Paint page Pearl Violet. Be careful not to move masks, let dry. Carefully remove masks. Glue painted circles on opposite page with gel medium. Glue marbles on top of each word with Diamond Glaze. Place gel medium on end of ribbon. Place ribbon between spine and signatures of book, let dry. Tie key to end of ribbon for a great bookmark.

Masking Words

by Laurie Goodson

Masked words are magic when magnified with flat back marbles.

1. Cover words with punched out circles.

2. Paint the page. Be careful to not move the circles.

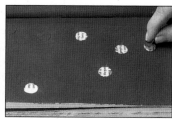

3. Remove the circles.

4. Adhere the flat back marbles with Diamond Glaze.

Masking Words
by Laurie Goodson

Bright watercolors and folded shapes result in pages that are simple but effective.

Purple & Orange Pages

SUPPLIES: Scraps of text weight paper • Dr. Ph. Martin Radiant concentrated Watercolor (Violet, Orange) • Paintbrush • 3 cups of water • 3M Repositionable glue stick • Gel medium
INSTRUCTIONS: On 3 different pages, mask words or phrases using scrap paper and glue stick. Paint pages with watercolors. Do not get paint under masks. Fold first 2 pages into triangles and glue with gel medium.

Poetry dog tags tied to the ends of satin ribbon make a wonderful page marker for these Blue and Pearl White brushed pages.

Blue Pages

SUPPLIES: Definition of an angel text ripped from an old dictionary • Two poetry dog tags • 7" piece of Light Blue and 8" piece of Medium Blue 1/8" satin ribbon • Lumiere paint (Blue, Pearl White) • Paintbrush • Gel medium
INSTRUCTIONS: Paint 2 pages with Blue and add a second coat of Pearl White, let dry. Glue definition on bottom of page with gel medium. Glue ribbon pieces between spine and signatures of book. Tie dog tags to ends of ribbon.

I just started playing with these decorative buttons and I see great possibilities. I think you will, too!

Pink Folded Pages

SUPPLIES: Small scrap of text weight paper • Handprint • Decorative pronged buttons • Lumiere paint (Halo Pink Gold, Pearl Blue) • Needle-nose pliers • 3M repositionable glue stick • Gel medium
INSTRUCTIONS: Find a phrase or word on the page that you want to stand out. Tear a piece of text weight paper to cover phrase or word. Apply repositionable glue to one side and place over phrase or word. Paint 2-page spread Halo Pink Gold, being careful not to move the mask. Let paint dry.

Now for the fun part... Round up a subject with a small hand, press hand in Pearl Blue paint and place hand on top of mask so the word or phrase is centered beneath hand. Carefully lift hand to avoid smearing. Once handprint has dried, remove mask. Fold opposing page, bottom outside corner up to spine, top outside corner down to spine. Using gel medium, glue folds down. Attach pronged buttons to corners and bend prongs down with pliers.

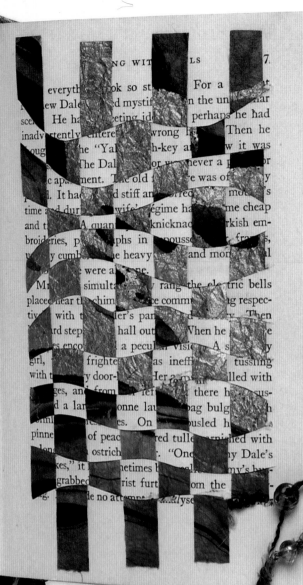

He mounted the steps, detached a small "Yale" latch-key from his watch chain and, after a vigorous ring which remained unanswered, opened the door himself.

Such action constituted part of a fixed routine. Being extremely impatient, he never waited for the butler to let him in. It was as much as Charles could do to get from his pantry to the hat-rack before the ponderous door had closed behind the master of the house. This evening Charles had not even got to the hat-rack. Mr. Dale waited ten seconds, then took his coat off laboriously. "Is the man sick, I wonder?" said he, and walked down the hall into the dining-room. Before him stood a large shining disk of mahogany. In the centre was placed one large loving-cup in silver-gilt, but the table was otherwise unset. "Damn!" said Mr. Dale. "I'm certain Amy didn't tell me that we were dining out; I'm sure I never said that I would go out tonight." Aggrieved, he walked back into the front hall, which looked unusually empty and made him remember to be angry again with Charles. Then he pushed open the door which led into his wife's drawing-room and entered.

Mrs. Dale had a passion for soft lamp and candle light, but this evening neither sconce nor taper was illumined. Mr. Dale switched on the central electric chandelier, and the room was flooded with garish brilliance. Was it the unaccustomed blaze which

Paper Weaving

Paper Weaving Page   *by Laurie Goodson*

SUPPLIES: Decorative text weight paper • Craft knife • Cutting mat • Ruler • Gel medium
INSTRUCTIONS: Glue 2 pages of book together, let dry. Place cutting mat beneath pages. Using craft knife, cut 11 wavy lines horizontally down page about ½" apart. Be sure not to cut to the edge of page. Cut decorative paper into ½" strips. Weave strips vertically in and out of cuts. Glue ends of strips to page with gel medium to secure.

Use a weaving technique you learned in grade school to give textural interest and visual drama to any book. The results are spectacular!

1. Place a cutting mat behind page and cut horizontal wavy lines with a craft knife.

2. Cut ½" strips of paper and weave through the horizontal cuts.

3. Glue ends of paper to the page to secure.

Paper Weaving

Da Vinci Pages

by Betsy McLoughlin

SUPPLIES: Decorative paper with Da Vinci designs • Black and Brown tissue paper • Assorted fibers • 9 Gold eyelets • Black ink • Eyelet setter • Hammer • Craft knife • Cutting mat • Xyron machine • 1/8" hole punch • Ultimate glue

INSTRUCTIONS: Using direct to paper technique, randomly apply ink to left page. Rip tissue paper, crinkle, smooth out and glue on page. Cut out pieces of decorative paper and glue in place.

On opposite page, crinkle decorative paper, smooth out, run through Xyron machine and adhere to page. Trim excess with craft knife and cutting mat. Using direct to paper technique, randomly apply ink to page.

Punch holes down edges of pages. Insert eyelets in left page. Lace eyelets and holes with fibers.

Ribbon Weaving Page

by Laurie Goodson

SUPPLIES: Seven 6" pieces of 1/4" Green ribbon • Craft knife • Cutting mat • Ruler • Gel medium

INSTRUCTIONS: Glue 2 pages of book together, let dry. Place cutting mat under pages. Using craft knife, cut straight lines horizontally across page. The sample has 11 cuts 1/2" apart. Do not cut to edge of page. Weave ribbon vertically in and out of cuts. Glue ends of ribbon on page to secure.

Fiber & Paper Weaving Page

by Laurie Goodson

SUPPLIES: Decorative text weight paper • Blue and Purple fibers • 8 Blue beads • 1/8" hole punch • Craft knife • Cutting mat • Ruler • Gel medium

INSTRUCTIONS: Glue 2 pages of book together, let dry. Place cutting mat beneath pages. Using craft knife, cut 11 wavy lines horizontally down page about 1/2" apart. Do not cut to edge of page. Cut decorative paper into 1/2" strips. Weave strips vertically in and out of cuts. Weave Blue and Purple fibers with one row of decorative paper. Glue ends of strips to page with gel medium to secure.

Cut 4 to 7 pages at an angle from top to bottom. Cut the next 4-7 pages at the same angle from bottom to top. Punch holes down sides of cut pages. Lace a Blue and a Purple fiber through holes and add beads to ends of fibers.

Keys & Tags Page

SUPPLIES: 3 large tags • Colorbox pigment ink (Stucco, Brown) • 9 flat metal keys • Waxed linen thread • Gel medium • Diamond Glaze

INSTRUCTIONS: Age edges of tags with pigment ink. Adhere keys to tags with glaze. Attach waxed linen thread to tags with lark's head knots. Glue tags onto the page.

RED PE...

wasn't Amy, by a lo...
and my patients m...
charming personali...
Amy wrote she co...
hasty scrawl of reg...
for her services, a...
comprehending,...
thought of her. E...
of things that I ov...
by no means a scr...
much we both t...
my own apprecia...
I felt she would...
sort of gorgeou...
such times and...
love.

To-day Amy...
after four yea...
asked Miss Ca...
an old friend a...
she surprised...
She'd been a...
have called "r...
any more, pro...
sweet faced, s...

was not only my office nurse, but she used to work opposite me at the operating table whenever I couldn't be sure of the right man. I used her for a special type of cases—I won't bother to go into that. But she was great stuff, and I prized her very highly —and was mostly in too much of a hurry to tell her so.

She left me about four years ago. She'd been taken ill while at her own home, a long way off, on a short vacation. I filled her place with considerable success—got a bright, intelligent young nurse, who

144

Tag Art
by Laurie Goodson

Tags in various sizes and shapes become a great art form when used as backgrounds or embellishments

Metal keys, rubber stamps and fibers add to the unusual look of these wonderful altered book pages.

1. Stamp both sides of the shipping tags with Fresco stamp pad.

2. Align tags and stamp design in the center.

3. Attach fibers to tags with lark's head knots.

4. Glue the tags in place.

More Tag Art
by Laurie Goodson

Angel on Tags Pages

SUPPLIES: 3 shipping and 3 small tags • Small Brown paper bag • 3 coin envelopes • Ivory paper • Rubber stamps (*Acey Deucy* angel, *Stamp Out Cute* map, *Limited Editions* key, pen tip, word) • Sepia archival ink • Fresco ink (Tuscan Earth, Sicilian Spice, Blue Grotto, Da Vinci Violet) • Memories Art Print Brown ink • Fibers • Small Brass clock charm • Gel medium

INSTRUCTIONS FOR ANGEL PAGE: Tear 2 pages of book leaving about 1½". Rub Tuscan Earth ink on front and back of tags. Placing tags so they touch, stamp angel with Sepia ink. Place glue in between 2 book pages and insert tags. Tie fibers on tags with lark's head knots and glue and charm on center tag.

INSTRUCTIONS FOR POCKET PAGE: Tear 2 pages behind angel page leaving 1½". Rub Fresco Sicilian Spice ink on paper bag. Stamp map with Art Print Brown. Glue bag between pages. Stamp map on Ivory paper with Art Print Brown. Fold accordion style and insert in bag.

INSTRUCTIONS FOR ENVELOPE PAGE: Tear 2 pages behind pocket page leaving 1½". Rub coin envelopes with Da Vinci Violet and tags with Blue Grotto. Stamp tags with Limited Editions designs and Art Print Brown. Glue envelopes between pages. Attach fibers to tags with lark's head knots. Insert tags in envelopes.

Envelope Page

SUPPLIES: Three large tags • Coin envelope • Decorative text weight paper • Rubber stamps (*Treasure Cay* script, *A Stamp in the Hand* pear) • Cats Eyes ink pads (Chestnut, Merlot) • Memories Art Print Brown ink • Fresco Tuscan Earth ink • Gold tassel • Assorted fibers • Gel medium

INSTRUCTIONS: Rip 2 pages from book leaving about 1" of each page in book. Using direct-to-paper technique and Cats Eyes, apply colors to tags and envelope. Glue coin envelope between ripped pages. Stamp tags with script and Art Print Brown ink. Stamp pear on tags with Tuscan Earth ink. Rip decorative paper and glue on tags. Attach tassel through holes in all 3 tags with lark's head knot. Attach fibers through hole in bottom of envelope. Insert tags in envelope.

Serendipity Page

SUPPLIES: Two large and 3 small White tags • Dark Blue handmade paper • Rubber stamps (background, *Uptown Design* 'serendipity') • Ancient Page White and Foxglove ink • 5 poetry dog tags • 5 Clear glass flat back marbles • Lumiere Pearl Violet paint • 5 White and 6 Lavender eyelets • 5 Silver jump rings • Purple fiber • Eyelet setter • Hammer • Sea sponge • ⅛" hole punch • Diamond Glaze

INSTRUCTIONS: Using a dampened sea sponge, apply a wash of diluted Pearl Violet paint to page, let dry. Stamp serendipity on right page with White ink. Stamp tags with background stamp and Foxglove ink. Attach tags to page with White eyelets. Using glaze, attach marbles to tags. Tear 1" strip of Dark Blue paper and glue across lower edge of left page. Attach Lavender eyelets to bottom of right page. Attach jump rings to dog tags. Lace fiber through eyelets catching jump rings on dog tags.

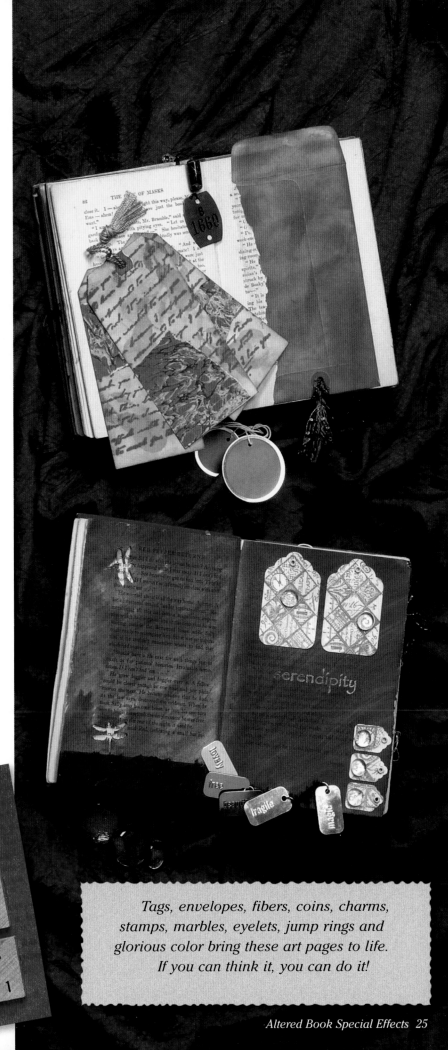

Tags, envelopes, fibers, coins, charms, stamps, marbles, eyelets, jump rings and glorious color bring these art pages to life. If you can think it, you can do it!

Making Layers

by Laurie Goodson

Rainbow Tab Pages

SUPPLIES: 6 small tags • *Stampers Anonymous* artistic mosaic rubber stamp • Colorbox Pinwheel pigment ink pad • Black Ancient Page ink pad • Gel medium

INSTRUCTIONS: Use 6 pages of book. Fold first page behind itself at about mid point and glue with gel medium. With each successive page, fold ¼" closer to outer edge. You should be able to see all 6 layers. Place a piece of paper behind first page to protect other pages when applying ink. Using Red pigment ink, color first page and one small tag. Color edge of next page and tag Orange. Repeat for other pages using colors of the rainbow. Don't forget to color one tag to match each ink. Let tags dry. Stamp tags with mosaic images and Black ink. Attach each tag to matching page starting near top of first page and working down to create a cascade of tabs and colorful pages.

Fold down a few pages, color them... the results give you a rainbow background for adding tags or objects from nature.

1. Fold and glue the pages.

2. Color the small tags and folded pages.

3. Stamp design on the tags.

4. Glue the tags in place.

Making Layers

by Laurie Goodson

This is a very easy method. Measure, cut and glue rainbow colored papers to trimmed book pages. Voila! A Rainbow Page!

Rainbow Page

SUPPLIES: Six handmade papers in rainbow colors • Craft knife • Cutting mat • Gel medium
INSTRUCTIONS: Cut each piece of paper the height of book page. Cut first piece to a width of 2" and each remaining piece ½" wider than previous piece for a layered effect. Using 2 pages of book for every piece of cut paper, cut pages about 1" wide with craft knife and cutting mat leaving a wavy edge. Glue pieces of paper between 1" pages starting with the narrowest and ending with the widest.

Metallic paint in Gold, Copper and Olive Green adorn these layered pages. Finish with words cut from text pages and glued to tags. Attach tags to page with eyelets.

Layered Pages

SUPPLIES: Words cut from text pages • Five small Accu-Cut tag die-cuts • Red cardstock • Lumiere paint (Metallic Gold, Super Copper, Metallic Olive Green) • 5 Red eyelets and washers • Eyelet setter • Hammer • Gel medium
INSTRUCTIONS: Use 5 pages of book. Fold first half of page back and glue. With each successive page, fold ¼" to ½" closer to outer edge. The last page will not be folded. You should be able to see all layers. Place a piece of paper behind each page to protect other pages when you are painting. Color the edge of third page with Metallic Gold paint. Use Super Copper on second page. Repeat with Metallic Olive Green on last page. Glue one cut-out word on each tag. Use eyelets to attach tags to first page. Glue first and second pages together.

Dreams Pages

SUPPLIES: 6 Clear self-adhesive file folder tabs with paper inserts • PSX dragonfly stickers • Skeleton leaves • Fresco ink (Olive Grove, Vesuvian Ash, Sicilian Spice, Blue Grotto, Vatican Wine, Da Vinci Violet) • Craft knife • Cutting mat • Gel medium
INSTRUCTIONS: Cut 1½" off right edge of 6 pages. Color each page a different color with Fresco inks using direct-to-paper technique. Add one tab to outside edge of each page, staggering tabs so all tabs are visible. On each paper insert, type, write or print a letter to spell DREAMS. Insert paper in tabs. Apply dragonfly stickers and glue skeleton leaves randomly on pages.

SUPPLIES: Ivory and Rust cardstock • Ivory paper • Assorted fibers • Rubber stamps (*Hero Arts* square shadow, *Stampers Anonymous* king, queen and pawn, *Magenta* square design) • Memories Art Print Brown dye ink • Sepia archival ink pad • Fresco ink pads (Amaretto Truffle, Tuscan Earth) • ¼" hole punch • Gel medium

INSTRUCTIONS: Stamp checkerboard pattern on 2-page spread using square shadow stamp and Sepia ink. Using square design stamp and Art Print Brown ink, stamp each Sepia square. On cardstock, stamp 7 pawns, one king and one queen Art Print Brown. Cut out chess pieces. Using pop-up base pattern, cut base from Rust cardstock and strips from Ivory. Glue chess pieces on strips and base. Glue strips on base and base to top of page at a slight V angle so pages will close flat. Using cardstock, a computer and printer, create tags with your choice of words. The tags shown say 'Checkmate!' and 'Imagination is more important than knowledge. Albert Einstein'. Cut a small rectangle around printed text, cut corners off of one end and punch a ¼" hole on that end to make tags. Age tags with Fresco inks. Tie fibers through holes in tags with lark's head knots. Glue tags on checkerboard page.

Pop-Ups are fun and easy to make and add a delightful sense of fun to themed pages. You'll love making these surprise action-filled projects.

Babies in Pots

by Betsy McLoughlin

SUPPLIES: Lattice print paper • Baby images from calendar • Scissors • Bone folder • Xyron machine

INSTRUCTIONS: Cut lattice paper to fit pages in book. Run paper through Xyron machine and adhere paper to pages. Cut out baby images. Select image that you want to pop up when book is opened. Fold image in half and then fold each side of image to form tabs. Glue tabs on page. Glue remaining images in place.

Pop-Up Pages

1. Stamp checkerboard pattern on page.

2. Continue the pattern on the second page.

3. Stamp the chess pieces on cardstock.

Heart Pop-Up Pages

by Laurie Goodson

SUPPLIES: Ivory cardstock • Text weight paper for masking • Rubber stamps (*Magenta* heart, *Inkadinkado* right and left wings) • Archival Sepia ink • Colorbox Gold Rush Metallic ink • Lumiere paints (Super Copper, Metallic Gold) • Paintbrush • 3M repositionable glue stick • Gel medium

INSTRUCTIONS: Using glue stick and strips of text weight paper, mask phrases and words on 2-page spread. Paint pages Super Copper and Metallic Gold, let dry. Carefully remove masks. Stamp heart on Ivory cardstock with Sepia ink. Make a mask and cover heart. Stamp wings repeatedly on each side to create large wings. Practice this technique on scrap paper before working on book. Remove mask carefully. Cut out heart and wings. Using pattern, cut pop-up base from Ivory cardstock. Paint pop-up Super Copper and Metallic Gold. Fold heart and wings in half, unfold and attach to base. Cut out a piece of Ivory cardstock and adhere to back of pop-up to add strength.

Peacock Pop-Up

by Betsy McLoughlin

SUPPLIES: Peacock image from magazine • White cardstock • Multi color yarn • Alphabet game tiles • Gold spray paint • Spray matte finish • Bone folder • Paintbrush • Ultimate glue

INSTRUCTIONS: Spray paint both pages Gold, let dry. Spray both pages with finish to seal, let dry. Cut out image and glue on cardstock. This will make the image stronger to withstand wear and tear. Fold image in half with bone folder. Fold image on each side to form tabs. Glue tabs on page applying glue with paintbrush. Arrange yarn on page, glue in place and let dry. Select Scrabble tiles to spell 'timeless' and glue on page.

4. Cut out the chess pieces leaving tabs on the bottoms.

5. Glue chess pieces on the base.

Origami Bowl Pages

SUPPLIES: Magenta text weight paper (2 sheets Purple, 2 sheets Lime Green) • Three small shipping tags • *Inkadinkado* word rubber stamp • Cat's Eye ink pads (Lime Green, Lavender) • Decorative flower shaped paper clip • Butterfly charm • Xyron machine • Diamond Glaze

INSTRUCTIONS: Cut and tear one Purple and one Lime Green sheet to cover parts of page. Run paper through Xyron and adhere paper to pages. Using direct-to-paper technique, rub Cat's Eye ink directly on tags. Stamp word on tags. Attach tags to page with paper clip. Fold origami bowl using Magenta text weight paper. Attach charm to bottom of bowl with Diamond Glaze. Using gel medium, glue bowl to page. Be sure to fold the bowl flat before closing book.

For origami bowl, cut 6" x 9" pieces of Lime Green and Purple text weight paper. Run papers through Xyron machine and press wrong sides together. Fold bowl following diagrams.

Folded 'Bowl' or 'Box'

by Laurie Goodson

What an unexpected delight! A colorful origami bowl that folds flat when you want to close your book.

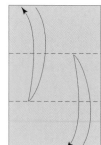 **1.** Make marks to divide paper in thirds. Fold, crease and unfold top and bottom.

2. Fold bottom edge up to middle crease. Fold top edge back to creased edge.

3. Your paper will look like this. Fold top edge down to creased edge.

4. Your paper will look like this. Fold bottom edge up to creased edge.

5. Your paper will look like this. Fold bottom edge up.

6. Bring the top layer corners down to meet the center fold line, crease. Repeat with other corners.

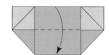 **7.** Fold top layer down.

 **8.** Your paper will look like this. Fold top layer down .

 9. Your paper will look like this. Fold all corners to center and crease.

 10. Your paper will look like this. Fold first layer up.

 **11.** Your paper will look like this. Grasp center of inside folds, pull up and out until flat. Squash and crease making 2 new points.

 **12.** Your paper will look like this. On outside, squeeze 2 points allowing paper to pop into bowl shape.

Journey Pages

by Laurie Goodson

SUPPLIES: Old map • Glassine envelope • Postage stamps • Travel stickers • An old photograph • Magazine clippings • 3 Gold photo corners • Gel medium

INSTRUCTIONS: Starting with largest clippings, cover entire 2-page spread. Mount photo with photo corners. Glue envelope at top of page and insert postage stamps. Cut old map into three 8" squares. Fold each square into Flower Fold. Create a chain by stacking and gluing squares together. Glue first square on page.

Flower Fold

Flower fold a map with dream destinations and add it to a page filled with memories of journeys past.. Clever you!

Fold three 8" squares

  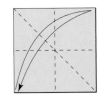   

1. Fold the square in half vertically, crease and open.
2. Fold in half horizontally, crease and open.

3. Fold in diagonally to make a large triangle, crease and open.

4. Bring opposite corners together and sides in to create a 4" square.

5. Turn squares as shown. Stack and glue the three 4" folded squares together.

6. Glue stack to book page. Fold back top corner and crease, creating pull to open map.

1. Glue set of 2 pages together. Spray paint the pages.

2. Cut strips across the page with a craft knife and ruler.

3. Tear out words and color the edges with a stamp pad.

4. Attach the eyelets to the metal tags.

5. Glue tags on words and words on strips.

A Little Word Play

by Laurie Goodson

Children of all ages will have hours of fun making different sentences with this word play design.

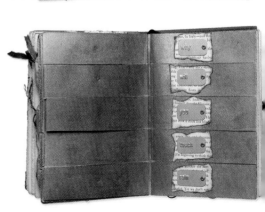

Dog Tags Pages

SUPPLIES: Scrap book pages • Cat's Eye Chestnut Brown ink pad • Photo • 4 Gold photo corners • 25 Poetry dog tags • 25 Copper eyelets • Eyelet setter • Copper spray paint • 1/8" hole punch • Hammer • Craft knife • Cutting mat • Gel medium
INSTRUCTIONS: To strengthen pages, glue 5 sets of 2 pages together. Spray paint facing page and 2-page spreads, making sure you cover other pages to protect book. Let dry. With dog tags, make 5 sentences using 5 dog tags for each sentence. Keep in mind the sentence can change because each word will be on a separate page. Using scrap book pages, tear out 25 small rectangles. Rub Chestnut Brown ink along edges of each piece. Using hole punch and eyelets, attach a dog tag to each piece of book page that you have torn and edged with ink. Using cutting mat and craft knife, divide painted pages into 5 equal strips. Place cutting mat under top page and cut from spine of book to outer edge. When done, you will have 5 little pages, one page for each dog tag. Repeat for 4 other pages. Glue dog tags on pages making sure sentences make sense reading from top to bottom. Mount photo with photo corners.

Dragonfly Pages

SUPPLIES: Decorative dragonfly paper • Three dragonfly die-cuts • Small glassine envelope • Text words cut from book pages • Xyron machine • Gel medium
INSTRUCTIONS: Measure and cut dragonfly paper to size of 2-page spread in book. Run paper through Xyron machine and apply to pages. Glue envelope on corner of page. Fill envelope with cut-out words. Glue dragonfly die-cuts on page with one flying out of envelope. Using cut-out words, make 2 sentences. Glue each sentence behind dragonflies to create a trail.

'S' Pages

SUPPLIES: Ivory cardstock • Large vinyl letter sticker • Chopstick or skewer • Two poetry dog tags with words beginning with S • Black rattail cord • Xyron machine • Gel medium
INSTRUCTIONS: On computer type every 'S' word you can think of and print on Ivory cardstock. Cut cardstock so it fits 2-page spread of book. Depending on the size of book, you may need 2 pieces of cardstock. Run cardstock through Xyron machine and adhere to pages. Peel backing off letter and press on corner of page. Glue 2 pieces of cord in gap between signatures and spine of book. Tie dog tags on cords.

'h' Page

SUPPLIES: Large vinyl self adhesive letter 'h' • Gold vellum • Xyron machine
INSTRUCTIONS: Press letter on page. Print a list of words beginning with 'h' on Gold vellum. Cut vellum to size. Run vellum through Xyron and adhere to page over letter.

Flag Pages

SUPPLIES: 6" x 11" piece of Beige cardstock • Twelve 1½" x 4" strips of decorative text weight paper for flags • Fresco Tuscan Earth ink • Gold tassel • ¼" hole punch • Gel medium

INSTRUCTIONS: Using direct to paper technique, rub Tuscan Earth ink on 2-page spread. Accordion fold cardstock every 1⅜". With gel medium, apply paper strips to cardstock, 2 strips per fold alternating direction of strips. Attach one end of accordion fold to book with gel medium Punch hole in opposite end of folded cardstock. Attach tassel through hole with lark's head knot. When you pull tassel end out, strips should lie semi-flat allowing you to see all of them.

Flag Pull-Out
by Laurie Goodson

Try your hand at making pull-out flags. Use different colors of paper or cut a photo into strips. The possibilities are endless!

1. Glue the paper strips in the accordion folds.

2. Glue strips on the opposite side of the next fold.

3. Continue gluing strips on alternating sides of the folds.

4. Glue completed flags on book's pages.